LOVE POEMS

LOVE POEMS

LOIS WYSE

Galahad Books / New York

First Galahad Book edition published in 1995.

Galahad Books

A division of Budget Book Service, Inc.

386 Park Avenue South

New York, NY 10016

Galahad Books is a registered trademark of Budget Book Service, Inc.

Published by arrangement with Garrett Press.
Library of Congress Catalog Card Number: 95-79471
ISBN: 0-88365-929-8

Book design by Cindy LaBreacht.
Printed in Hong Kong

Contents

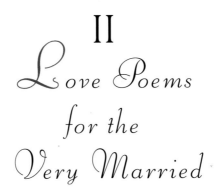

For a love that lasts.

I

Love Poems
for a
Rainy Day

Dr. Thinkgood

At a dinner party the other evening
I was seated next to a surgeon.
We dissected wines and politics
And finally we got around to women.
I know about the man/woman thing, he said.
    (Everybody does, Doctor).
But I really know.
I had to get married twice to find out.
The first time
I was married to a woman
Who said she would have loved me more
If my politics were different.

Now I am married to a woman
Who doesn't even know my politics.

She just gets pleasure out of me.
She loves loving me.
Isn't that simple?

Sometimes I reach out and touch her
Just because it makes me feel good.
A good marriage is simply feeling good.
It is pleasing yourself.
It really doesn't have a thing to do with
Politics or religion or who makes the bed.
My first wife?
Well, she married a man who is so conservative
He makes dull old me look like a card-carrying radical.

But you know something?
I don't think my first wife even sees the difference.
I realize now that it wasn't my politics she didn't love.
It was me.
And when you get to the point in life
When you know you're not right for someone
Well, then you've really grown up.

And you have the hurt to prove it.

Hello Sunshine

It rained last night,
That warm-washed rain of summertime
And other times
When you and love were here.

Did it rain on your life, too, last night?
And if it did
Were you awake to hear
And to remember
All the times that we held close
As another storm blew past?

I must tell you something, dear.
I no longer am afraid of rain,
For now I know
That no love but the one
That outlasts wet and weary times
Can be
The sunshine love of life.

The Opportunity for Love

A small brown wren she
Who said, "I never had
The opportunity for love."

Ah, little bird,
It is not
Opportunity
That creates love.

It is
Imagination.

Single Woman

Don't feel sorry for me.
In lots of ways
I like
The singleness of me.

I like
Watching TV,
Reading good books,
Washing my hair at 4 AM,
Playing any music I want
. . . and getting the whole bed.

I hate
Eating alone in restaurants,
Buying one ticket for the movies,
Going to bridal showers,
Listening to my mother
    ("Why isn't he good enough?"
    "You ought to see the nice man she married.")
. . . and Sunday.

I hope
Somewhere around the corner
I will find someone
Who will let me
Hold on to all I like,
Get rid of all I hate,
And nourish the essential me.

What scares me
Is that I might go
From single to zero
In marriage.

Social Commentary

Ridiculous, the dinner guests agreed.
Absolutely ridiculous
That a woman her age
Be so—well, so obviously—involved
With a man his age.

"Besides, he's not even good-looking."
"Of course, she isn't either."
"But at least he's young."

Ah, my charming dinner guests
(Who count calories and birthdays,
Who measure men in dollars and in dividends)
Can you last remember
When anyone of any age
Seemed so—well, so obviously—involved
With you?

$\mathcal{L}$esson

It is so painful
To learn when to love.
But it is even more painful
To learn when not to love.

The Other Woman

For a woman who is supposed
To do a lot of loving,
I sometimes do
A lot of hating.

I hate me for being so involved with him.
I hate him for not being involved enough with me.
I hate them for needing him.
It's all so—oh, so unloving.
And I never meant it to be that way.

All I wanted was a little love,
And it certainly started innocently enough.
But on our way to finding love
We lost our innocence.

When things get really intense between us
We touch and listen to music,
And we are so close and so much a part of each other
That we shut out all the rest of the world,
And he promises that some way we are going to live together,
And I cry and ask when.
And he holds me close and says, "Someday."

Someday I can go to his business dinners,
And someday those tickets I order for the theater will be for us,
Not for them.
Someday I'll be able to call him in the middle of the day,
And he'll drop everything to find out what's bothering me.
The way it is now I can't afford to tell him what's bothering me
Because he loves the no bother of me.
No stopped sinks in our relationship.
He adores the reality of our unreality.
But someday…
Someday, he says.

I don't know what will happen
If I tell him we're through.
I'm not sure I'm strong enough
To eat alone every night,
And I'm not sure I'm brave enough
To get into a bed that's cold on both sides.

And as much as I love
Meeting him at five
And dread
His leaving me at seven,
What would I do without those two hours?

What do I want?
Part-time Charlie
Or full-time, empty me?

I wish I knew what to do.

How do you know when
You want to change your life
And upset a clutch of people
In order to make yourself happy?

When do you decide
You have the right to decide?

More important…
When does he?

One, Two.

Single people
Are lonely and unhappy
Much of the time.

Just like
Married people.

Hearth-To-Hearth

So there you are.
Tired by the long distance run of now.
And here I am.
Tired by the pop pop pops of today.
And yet we know
That when we touch
You will forget the run
And all my little pops will slowly sputter
In the first quiet stirring
Of a rekindled love.

Trust Me

Here we are again.
You on one side of the bed,
I on the other.

You tightly bound by skepticism.
I freed by trust.

Know something, love?
I'd rather be me.

Maybe trusting someone too much
Causes pain tomorrow...
But, oh, what a nice today.

Divorced Woman

I'm getting a divorce.
Now maybe that news doesn't knock you out,
But it's tearing me up in little pieces.

To begin,
I always thought
Divorce, like marriage,
Was a private affair.
Well, it's not.
When you get a divorce
It's not just you and him.
It's his family and yours,
Friends, the people you work with, neighbors.
Hell, even the dry cleaner has an opinion.

In the beginning my friends came to see me.
It was like making a condolence call.
Everybody was looking around for the body,
But he had taken his body
To Palm Springs.

One friend told me
. . . After all, who but a dear friend would tell you. . .
That the story around town
Was that my husband
Was in love with another woman.

Another said she'd heard
I had a boy friend.
Oh my God, what a deadly expression.
A boy friend at my age.
Couldn't it at least be a lover?

One friend called to say
She didn't know how she and her husband
Would manage without us.
Her husband called and said the same thing.
Are we supposed to be the glue
For a lot of unstuck marriages?

Another friend said
She took tranquilizers and went to bed for two days.
And after a week of informing people,
I got to the point
Where I couldn't tell anyone
Because I couldn't stand seeing
The hurt on their faces.

What nobody realized was that
Underneath all that talk of
Alimony, custody and child support,
That beneath the surface of sympathetic clucking
There was a very scared woman
Who was falling apart.

Me.

A Good Love
Works Because
A Good Love
Works

There really is no pattern
To a love that works.
Do her neuroses
Fit his psychoses?
Does his spaghetti
Match her sauce?
Don't ask me, my dear.

All I know for sure
Is that our love still works
So long as you can tell me
We are going to have two whole days together
. . . and I am glad.

Equal Rights

See that man? my friend inquired.
His wife left him two years ago,
And he still has not recovered.

I shook my head in disbelief.
You mean men hurt as much as women do?

$\mathcal{H}$onestly

You do not lie.
Oh no, you never lie.
Instead you cut
A careful pattern
And refit the truth
To fit your reasons.

You know, my dear,
There are times
I would prefer
A good, fat lie.

$\mathcal{L}$ast $\mathcal{W}$ords

Look, she said,
I just can't stand it
One minute longer.

       What?

I'm leaving.
I'm getting out.
I'm through.

       Because just once
       I had an affair?

Yes.

       But I don't love her.
       I swear.
       All I did was
       Go to bed with her.
       I do not love her.

That, my dear,
Is why I am leaving.
You see, I could have stayed
If you had loved her.

Keeping Time

Nine days away.
You are nine days away.
Time. It moves   s   o   s   l   o   w.

One day away.
You are one day away.
Time. Itdoesnotmove.

The Cocktail Party

Are you married, he asked.
Yes, she answered,
But I'm not fanatic about it.

Of course not.
Nobody today is fanatic about marriage.
Nowadays we are fanatic about
Upstairs/Downstairs
Gold bullion
And new apartments.

After all,
Over a glass of white wine and two canapes
Who wants to hear it for something your mother likes?

Married Woman

I come from the old time
When marriage was the answer
To this, the new time,
When marriage is the question.

And, like many women in my world these days,
I wonder if there is something wrong with me
To want marriage
And not The Other Possibilities.

Possibilities that do not require
Commitment,
Hope
Or faith.

But what is life without the faith
That precedes commitment?
Is the road worth taking without the hope
That sustains despair?

A married woman learns
To rule the world
In the confines of her home,
In the shadows of her hope,
In the fire of her faith,
In commitment to her love.

Married?
Why am I married?

Caught in the sea
Of changing linens and changing attitudes,
Supervising the household of pepper mills and salt shakers?

Why am I married?

Because beyond the shifting winds and low-lying clouds
I have yet to see a sign
That anything but marriage
Is the future of mankind.

All Aboard

There is a small commuter train
That runs a fast and silent track
Between your mind and mine.

Somedays the train is overcrowded,
A lot of hangers-on,
Back to the bar car.

Then there are times when you may be
The solitary passenger
On the long and bumpy road to me.

And we both know the dreary days
When it would be
So easy to turn back.

Yet each time you have chugged on.
And although I do not always seem a grateful woman,
I really am so glad you bought
That one-way ticket a long, long time ago.

I Knew Her When She Was a Brunette

I have been married
A very long time.

And in that time
My husband
Has had three wives—
All of them
Me.

Understanding

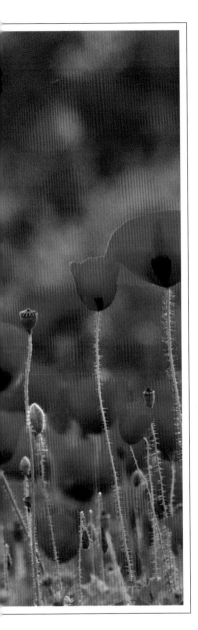

I do not know the words
Of that small song in my heart,
But somehow, my dear,
I think you do.

The Fidelity Gap

So many sounds to lure me
So many views to tempt me
So, for a moment, I may stray.

But it would not be natural
If I never heard the music
Of other violins
And never saw the view
Beyond the second story.

Human Sexual Response, etc.

You can take all the how-to books
And all the why-not literature,
Give them to all the lab technicians
And all the slide rule specialists,

And not one of them will ever know
The measure of trust
That goes into love—
Which is the only human response
No one has learned to measure.

Sometimes Imperfect, Often Impossible

You are
Sometimes imperfect,
Often impossible

And still I love you

Because, my sweet, you are
The only man in the world
Who makes me feel
At home in the world

Even though I am
Sometimes imperfect,
Often impossible

The Twentieth Century Man

J. D. is terribly rich
(Of course)
Except for
His guilt-edged insecurities.

The Widow

In the beginning
I would look at my watch and say,
"Yesterday he was here."

It has been a long time now since
I looked at my watch.
It has been so long
I do not even look at the calendar.

But in the beginning
People listened to each detail
As if listening confirmed their mortality.
They were still here at the end of the story.
I guess fresh grief is like fresh milk.
We consume it quickly before it sours.

But grief cannot be worn
Season after season
Like a string of pearls.

Mourning becomes an embarrassment
To those who watch
The seasons of our sorrow.

A well-behaved widow
Does not cry.
(Me? Cry? Just because
I am lonesome for
The only man I ever loved)

A good widow
Gets on with life
(I brush my teeth and do not beat
My hands against the wall. I never look up
From my needlepoint and ask, "Why?")

A proper widow
Knows her place.
(Of course, I understand that
You will invite me to the next party...
The one with women only)

A thoughtful widow
Makes no demands on children.
(I smile and tell them yes, go ahead.
I know you have your own life. I do not say
Once I had a life—)

I think now as I lie here in the dark
Of all the things we meant to do.
Alone they are nothing. But who wants
To listen to the solo song of widowhood?

No one but another widow, for she
Is the only one who knows the bitter truth.
It never gets better.
It only gets ordinary.

Need

The problem for those who love
Is those we love.
They are afraid
We need them too much.

And so we do.

But until we can stop our need
Long enough
To stop our love
They will never know
How much they need us.

And so they do.

The Perfect Child

She was the perfect child
Who marched to her mother's beat
A beat in time replaced by
Teacher, husband, children, job.

> Rat-a-tat
> Let's hear it for
> The four-square
> Ordered life.

Just a minute.
Who ordered life?
Not she.

She ordered beauty, dignity and reason.
(After all, she was the perfect child)
But what she got was life.

> She ordered out of
> Column A
> And what she got was
> Ratatouille.

She reordered the disorder

"Four wallet size
And enlarge two."

But somehow the enlargement
Was not as big as life itself
And she still could not find herself
On the fine-tuned screen.

What ever became of the order
Of her early four-square life?

Is it behind doors that do not open?
Flying out of windows that do not shut?

She speaks if anyone should ask:

She says that she is out.
Out of step,
Out of sorts,
And, in her perpetual confusion,
She is definitely
Out of order.

And her mother nods and says,
Ah, she was the perfect child.

Up the Up Escalator

She leaned and looked back
At the lanky form that lounged
Near the last step of the escalator.
Don't worry, she called,
The bitter taste won't last.

How do you know? he asked.

It never does with yogurt, she replied.

Do I dare tell her that it does
With almost everything else?

This and That

It rained again today,
And when I left
Coated, booted and umbrella-d,
People said,
You mean you're going out in that?

What they did not know,
My love, is
I went out in that
For this.

For my love with my love

II

Love Poems

for the

Very Married

I Think I Love You

Once, when we were very young,
You looked at me and said,
"I think I love you."
And I bristled slightly
(as young girls do).
And I said to you, "Think?
You only think you love me?
You mean you do not know?"

For at that moment I knew love.
I was on intimate terms with Cole Porter lyrics,
And I cried when I read *Wuthering Heights*.

But now that I have grown up
I know the timeless treasure of your words.
For love must have a way to grow,
And you found the way so long ago.
You took the time to think our love…
And still you do.
A good love takes thinking through.
And living with.
And I knew
The first morning I awoke and touched you next to me…
I, too, could say,
"I think I love you."

A Cozy Heart

Once I thought that love
Was tempestuous,
Tumultuous,
"Kiss me quick."

I was wrong.

Love is usually a very comfortable way of life,
A cozy heart,
Kisses on the cheek,
"Wear your rubbers and blow your nose."

And what keeps a love so cozy?
The fact that every so often love is
Tempestuous, tumultuous…
"Kiss me quick."

Nothing

I suppose it was something you said
That caused me to tighten
And pull away.
And when you asked,
"What is it?"
I, of course, said,
"Nothing."

Whenever I say, "Nothing,"
You may be very certain there is something.
The something is a cold, hard lump of
Nothing.

Zipped

How many times have you stood in the doorway
And watched while I
Zipped,
Gartered,
Fastened,
Buttoned,
Combed,
Mascaraed,
Tugged and pulled at
Me?

I do not know, my love.
I do not know how many times.
But please, my sweet, don't ever turn your head.

Heart-To-Heart

There is a cord
Unseen
That binds us heart-to-heart.
The surest way
For me to shorten the cord
Is to let you choose the length.

For if I choose to tighten
That unseen cord
By poking,
Prying,
Wondering,
Why?-ing,
You will dissolve the cord
And create
An unseen wall
For both of us to see.

And that, my beloved,
Would be the tragedy
Of this
Or any
Marriage.

Possessed

Remember once
I said to you,
"I'm not a possessive woman."
(I was wearing the white lace robe at the time.)
"I'll never try to own you."
(That night it was the pale green with black lace.)
"Darling, you're free. You're loose. You are your own man."
(The blue shift it was. The one with bows on the shoulders.)
"Dearest, of course you don't have to meet me. It's your choice."
(Pale pink, I think, with a diaphanous skirt.)
"I waited for your call, my love."
(Two bows in my hair…white mules on my feet.)
I know I said I'm not possessive.
And when I said it
I wasn't I wasn't I wasn't.
Now, however, I am a very possessive woman.
(And I can't remember what I'm wearing.)

Yes

"Do you still want me?" you asked.
And I said, "You don't have to ask me every day."
You said, "Well, do you?"
And I said, "Yes."

But what I really said within my heart was,
"Want him?"
Do I want him?
In an exotic, quixotic way
I want him.
I want him because
I can walk with him,
And he talks to me about the things I like to talk about.
And he says funny things to me,
And sometimes he thinks they're so funny
He says them twice.
And I know him better than
Any woman has any right to know a man.
And with all that I find
Just when I think I know him best,
I know him not at all.
And all I really want is a chance to know him better,
And that takes time.
And I would like to take all the time given me
To know him better
Which is the real reason
I cannot bear to be away from him.
"Yes."

Sec

The waiter brought the wine to the table,
And you sipped it carefully,
Nodded slightly,
And went on saying what you were saying
Which was
"I love you."

And then you said,
"Now taste the wine.
It's very good, very dry."
Oh no, it's not my
Dear.
When you said,
"I love you,"
I tasted but the sweetest wine.

The Quicker
to See You
Again

We reached the corner of the street,
And you turned and walked away.
But not I.
I ran.
I ran from you as quickly as I could.
I felt your eyes upon my fast-retreating back
And knew that you kept turning 'round
To watch me run away.

But what you could not know
As I ran down the street
Was that I ran because
I cannot bear to walk away from you.

Just Then

The other day
You looked at me.
You did not say,
"I love you,"
But just then you believed it.

The Grand Ballroom of the Plaza Hotel

Our marriage was not made
In a chilly chapel,
Country church or
The Grand Ballroom of the Plaza Hotel.

For it was only long after the ceremony
That we learned
Why we got married
In the first place.

The Good Life

The other night
I was involved
In a discussion
Of the good life…
Whatever that is:
Four Seasons
   Balenciaga
      Firenze
Chablis
        A fireplace that works
         Chanel #5
   Two weeks in Acapulco
     Ice cream
Then someone mentioned
Love
And a man's great need for wife
Or mistress.

I moved back
Into my
Very own thoughts
And mentally echoed
The words of the speaker as he sipped his tea,
"A man's great need for wife or mistress."
And I silently said,
"Wife or mistress?
Oh, you poor man.
How sad it is you do not know
The Good Life is
One woman who is both."

Sunday

Sometimes
When we talk
I get the distinct feeling
You are not glad
You are you
I am me
And
We are we.

I detect a detached chill.

It used to worry me
Until I realized
That only a man
Who can be very attached
Can also be very detached.
And though at times I still detect detachment
I can weather it.
For I have come to learn that
You and I, my love,
Do not live in a temperate zone.

A State of Mind?

ESP?
Do I believe in ESP?
When you asked, I laughed and said,
"ESP? I don't even believe in CIA."
So maybe it wasn't such a good joke.
But don't you see...
I believe in ESP so much
I'm afraid to say I do.
I believe that when you are away
You know the times I'm frightened...
Or why would you call just
At the moment
The frantic, unsaid call for help is sent
From my mind to yours?
Why would you say,
"At three o'clock today
I thought of you."
Does the long arm of coincidence
Have a short life?
Can you believe that you and I
Are a state of mind?

My Toes Don't Curl

When I open the door
And see you there,
I don't hear bells,
My toes don't curl,
My heart does not beat faster.

Until later.

I Wish for You

I wish for you
Each small success
That makes a man a man.

I wish for you
An outside cut,
A twist of lime,
An order from the Coast,
A second look from pretty girls,
A second look for pretty girls,
And one glittering riposte.

I wish for you
Unshaven Sundays,
Brilliant Mondays,
And occasionally a day with nothing to do…
But ride waves or bikes or roller skates
And reflect, my dear, on
The importance of Not Being Corporate You.

Let others wish you
Hand-tailored suits,
English boots,
And dream executive dreams for you.
It is only money that they wish, my sweet,
But I want riches for you.

For an Out-of-Town Husband

Of course you have to travel.
All husbands have to travel,
But I thought you ought to know that
We are so married I know you by your telephone ring.
It is a short, impatient ring
Followed by a long,
"Hello how are the children did you have a good day?"
Then sometimes there is silence
Which is a very nice thing in a marriage.
And during that silence
We both say the most understanding things of all.

I Understand You Better Than You Think I Do

There they were:
The careful measured tones…
So clear that I could see them.
They precede always
Something important
That you will say.

So I closed my mind
And shut my ears
Because never yet have you
Said something joyous
In a
Something Important Voice.

Even now as I recall
The fragments of your thoughts
I am not sure just what you said,
But I am sure you meant
"No."

Half-Squeezed

Somewhere in the
Half-squeezed tube of toothpaste,
In the comb of mine
You use,
In the TV shows we lie and watch…
Somewhere in all of this
We sink our roots.

We draw our strength
In such strange ways.
We build our life
On toothpaste, combs, and
Television shows with highly predictable endings.

Central Park South

Sometimes when I'm not with you
I pretend I am,
And I walk through the park.
Do you know something...
It's really very dirty in the park.
I mean there are big old rubbish grinders
That roll down the paths
Stirring yesterday's dust all over today
And the benches aren't clean
And even the ducks look dirty.

But when I look
Across the lake
And see the rock
Where we sometimes sit,
The park looks bright once more.

I Just Talked to You on the Telephone

There is a certain tone
That creeps into your voice
From time to time.

Not demanding
Or impatient.
Insistent is the word,
I think.

A combination of
Male assertiveness
And possessiveness.

And I like it.

Lines to an Unhandy Man

You never made
A lamp base out of a Cracker Jack box,
An extra room out of an unused closet,
Or a garden out of a pile of clay.
All you ever made was
A woman out of me.

On Deposit in a Secret Heart

It's like money in the bank.
The delicate, off-balance, improbable things
    that happen in a moment…
The day you said you couldn't see me off,
Then at the last minute came to the station as the train
    was leaving
And raced the diesel along the track.
And I said, "It's just like the movies."
And you said, "Yes, it's just like the movies,"
And we kissed without ever touching.
Or the day…or the day…or the day…
All the delicate
Off-balance
Improbable things that happen in a moment
To be stored and treasured
On deposit in a secret heart…
Withdrawn when needed,
And redeposited for another rainy day.

Half Past Loving

It was very casual
And a game of sorts.
You covered the face of the clock
And told me to guess the time.
I guessed, and I was wrong.
As usual.
You guessed, and you were right.
As usual.

I didn't really know
Just what that proved
Until the day you covered the face of the clock
And guessed the time, and you were wrong.

And suddenly I knew
That made us right.

A Private Place

There is within each of us
A private place
For thinking private thoughts
And dreaming private dreams.

But in the shared experience of marriage,
Some people cannot stand the private partner.

How fortunate for me
That you have let me grow,
Think my private thoughts,
Dream my private dreams.

And bring a private me
To the shared experience of marriage.

Maybe I Unplugged the Phone

I started to write a poem to you,
And my pen ran dry.
My mouth ran dry.
My heart pounded.
"There is terrible significance in this,"
I thought.
I ran and found another pen
And wrote…
Not easily…
But I wrote.
"See, everything is still all right,"
I said to me.

Why didn't you call from Los Angeles today?

Do You Need Me?

Remember that day in New York?
You know, the last day we were there.
I had just bought the pink suit
(the one with the funny loops you like so much).
I walked out of the store,
And I saw one of those there-on-the-sidewalk phone booths
So I called the hotel for messages.
The operator read all the usual nothings.
And then she came to that message from you.
It said, "Do you need me? I'll be at…"
Funny.
I never heard where you'd be.
I heard only
"Do you need me?"
And I thought,
"Do I need you?"
And slowly I put the receiver back on the hook
And I said to myself…
Oh, how I need you.
This very moment I need you.
How dear you are. How right that you should show me what
"I love you"
Really means.

$\mathcal{N}on\text{-}\mathcal{S}top$

Someone asked me
To name the time
Our friendship stopped
And love began.

Oh, my darling,
That's the secret.
Our friendship
Never stopped.